An Acorn for Emily

The True Story of One Remarkable Squirrel

Anita Marie Rosinola and
Christine Rosinola Wittmann

authorHOUSE®

AuthorHouse™
1663 Liberty Drive, Suite 200
Bloomington, IN 47403
www.authorhouse.com
Phone: 1-800-839-8640

First published by AuthorHouse   12/15/2008

ISBN: 978-1-4389-3112-8 (sc)

Printed in the United States of America
Bloomington, Indiana

This book is printed on acid-free paper.

Cover Design, Art, Photography by Christine Rosinola Wittmann Additional photos Marr Bailey

Dedication

To Lisa Bakely, my friend, who introduced me to the world of squirrels and taught me all about them. She presented me with my first squirrel Peggy Sue and Emily who ultimately was the inspiration for this book.

To the late Gregg Bassett, President of the Squirrel Lover's club and pet squirrel owner for his understanding, encouragement and appreciation of my love for Emily. His untimely passing left a big void for the many friends, club members, and squirrels he so loved.

To my late parents for providing a household that was always blessed with a multitude of well loved pets.

To my sister Christine who helped write this book, provided artwork and photography, and who helped convey in words what was in my heart. I also thank her for the beautiful poem.

Contents

Chapter One

Humble Beginnings.....A Place of My Own

My story begins with my decision to find a place I
could really call home.   A place of my own.... the very
thought lifted my spirits as I sought to relocate to a
comfortable, modest house with a little privacy after years
of apartment living. It was the early 1980's and after a
long search I landed a townhouse in Blackwood, New
Jersey. For me, it was a great deal and the opportunity I'd
been waiting for. There was plenty of space and at last I
would have a back yard of my very own, a place to sit and
enjoy the birds and other wildlife I hoped would visit,
a quiet place to come to at the end of the day, my own
little piece of heaven. Feeding the birds had always been
a pleasure, watching them come and gratefully accept my
offerings of bread, seeds and leftovers from my dinner
plate. Now I started buying big bags of sunflower seeds,
cracked corn, and whatever else my budget would allow.
It didn't take long for the neighborhood squirrels to learn
there were "good eats" at my place. The squirrels soon
took over, leaving the birds little to eat as those whimsical
bushy-tailed characters cleaned up. Before long I found
myself throwing extra food and nuts on the ground for the

squirrels, in hopes they'd leave the birdfeeder full of seeds I'd set on my picnic table alone. But those aggressive blue jays honed in on the nuts, so it was an on-going battle to keep everyone happy and well fed, but I enjoyed watching them so much I kept the food coming. Word caught on fast in the neighborhood and each week brought more squirrels. It was as though they had some secret code amongst themselves! I could envision them chatting to each other, "Hey! We found a great place to hang out and this lady's actually feeding us nuts!! Peanuts, walnuts...all you can eat!!"

One day a particular little squirrel caught my eye. I'd named her Petie, not realizing that "he" was a "she!" Everyday she came to dine and soon became very friendly and trusting. The fences that separated the townhouses and gave me the privacy I so craved became her favorite places to perch and run along. When I called her name, she would perk up her ears and come flying across those fences to my yard. I learned to tell the males from the females so my Petie became "Peanut." Soon I had a name for each one that came to visit. There was Peanut of course, Himsey, Half Pint and Frenchie, to name a few. I could tell one from the other as though they were children, learning to identify them by markings on their tails, faces, or even by the length of their tails. They learned to trust me and soon were taking nuts from my hand. Peanut began climbing up my legs, sometimes taking the nut right from my mouth! The neighbors thought I was crazy and a few of them, unhappy with my feeding of the squirrels even threatened to harm them. I was always upset and afraid for my little friends. I loved how they followed me around the neighborhood, greeting me on my walks. No matter what the weather, I walked daily, often stopping at the little wooded area across the street from my house to feed and play with them. Peanut became my favorite and her name was so appropriate..... she loved her peanuts! Her trust of me deepened, so much so that when she had babies I'd find her bringing them around to my yard to show them off and let me feed them. I really came to love that squirrel. She was my best friend. To help accommodate her new family I placed nesting boxes high up in some trees. Watching the mother squirrels feed their young was truly a pleasure for me. Those little nesting boxes were well used! There seemed to always be a little head peeping out of the holes. It was humorous to see their curiosity grow and watch them get their "tree legs" as the careful mothers coached them in the fine art of becoming squirrels. It occurred to me that in all my years I'd paid so little attention to these fascinating creatures. Now here I was, feeding and caring for them, learning so much about their habits. I'd no idea they could be so entertaining! And entertain they surely did for every day was a new adventure and I was just captivated by them. I fell in love with these simple woodland creatures.

The family of squirrels in my yard was growing, and with it grew the confrontations with my neighbors who were anything but pleased about it. Some would try to shoot the squirrels with BB guns, and I soon found myself in court over the matter. Fortunately I won my case.

The disgruntled neighbor was not only fined and had his gun confiscated but also spent some time in jail. But this wasn't the end of my problems with neighbors and it became apparent I would have to start feeding my furry friends a bit farther a field, away from the people who would harm them. The squirrels followed me, so it was no trouble to entice them to go to the edge of the woods to eat.

Little Peanut started coming into my house to get her treats, and she always left with a few to take for "afters." She was an industrious little squirrel and one afternoon I found her pawing through the trash in search of papers for a nest. The idea occurred to me that some old socks might do the job nicely, so when she came to me I presented her with them. She rolled it up nicely in her mouth and scurried up the tree and placed it in her nest! It was the cutest thing to watch, and it made me feel good knowing I'd helped with her new house construction! The entire experience of feeding and helping these little creatures was wonderful for me and for them too. I wished it would be possible to actually have one for a pet, but I knew that wasn't fair. Like all wild creatures, squirrels need to be free to live and play in their own natural environment. Still, I longed to have one as a constant companion in my home. As a child growing up I recalled my mother taking in homeless and injured animals. Sometimes it was a bird, or some other wild creature. Though they may not have stayed long, mom usually managed to nurse the little invalid back to health enough to set it free. We never had a squirrel in our care, but that didn't mean there wasn't one out there somewhere that might need care. Someday, somewhere, there might be one that needed more help than could be given in the wild.

Chapter Two

Meeting Lisa

My prayers were answered one day when I noticed
a squirrel in my yard that didn't seem quite right. Not
wanting to get too close, I observed it from a distance
but wasn't sure if it was injured or just sick. There was a
wildlife refuge nearby and I called and asked their advice.
They put me in touch with a woman named Lisa. She
had been a volunteer for Animal Welfare for many years
and was raising and rehabilitating squirrels on a regular
basis. What luck! I called Lisa and told her all about my
little family of squirrels, about how much I loved caring
for them and especially about the one I was concerned for.
She gave me instructions on how to trap it humanely and
the appropriate place to take it for veterinary care. But as
I observed it over the next day or two, it seemed fine and
trapping became unnecessary.

Lisa was a fascinating person. We soon became the
best of friends and I found myself visiting her often to see
the many squirrels in her care. Most were babies that had
been abandoned when their mothers were killed. Lisa was
feeding them with an eyedropper and formula until they
were old enough to be released into the wild. I couldn't

get over how many she was caring for. They were adorable!
A few were not able to be released due to major medical
problems and they became her pets. Some were paralyzed
from their injuries, a couple were blind. They were kept in
spacious cages but were often let out to roam at will in the
house. Sometimes I'd see one sitting on the windowsills
or climbing on Lisa's back. I got such a kick out of Lisa
and those squirrels, and wished I could be doing the same
sort of humane work, though perhaps on a smaller scale.
Lisa was a person you couldn't help but love. She was
one of the kindest, sweetest people I'd ever met with a
heart as big as Texas. The welfare of those squirrels meant
everything to her. In the years that followed, I learned
a great deal from this very kind hearted and generous
friend.

Lisa definitely had a way with all animals. I was even
introduced to a woodchuck named Heidi, a creature she
had nursed back to health who decided to stay with Lisa
and her husband for a long time. Heidi didn't want to
leave! Lisa, her husband Dick and their son Richie were
all wonderful with animals. I'm sure Heidi sensed that
too, and her decision to stay with this loving family was
a happy arrangement for all concerned. Not all of the
animals in Lisa's care survived, but they were given the
very best of care and a chance for survival they otherwise
never would have had. Lisa gave her all for her animal
friends be they chipmunk, squirrel, woodchuck, possum
or anything else that needed care. But when it came to
those squirrels, she was a book of knowledge. A couple of
years into our friendship I told Lisa one day that I would

love to have a squirrel of my very own to love and care for, and that if ever she found another one that couldn't be released into the wild because of a permanent disability I would be so grateful if she'd let me care for it. My chance finally came when Lisa called one day with a baby squirrel that had been brought to her. The little creature was paralyzed and could not use its hind legs. Would I like to try and take care of it? Would I? Of course I jumped at the opportunity! I fell in love with the tiny squirrel from the moment I saw it! Lisa kindly showed me how to feed it with an eyedropper, mixing Gerber rice cereal with a little whole milk and special vitamins from the vet. I would warm the formula slightly and give it to the squirrel every couple of hours or so around the clock for several weeks until it could eat on its own. Then its diet would move on to nuts, fruits, veggies, acorns, greens and anything I could find outside that squirrels liked. Branches and twigs were brought in for the little tike to chew on. I found soft blankets and stuffed animals to make my new companion more comfortable. Eventually I had a custom made cage to house her, a roomy 3 x 3 foot square and 3 feet high. Lisa had shown me how to fashion a hammock at the top of the cage for her to sleep in. Her son had found a long sturdy branch which served as a way for her to climb into her hammock whenever she wanted to sleep. I named my little friend Peggy Sue. At this time in my life I also had a marmalade cat named Morris and a Scottish terrier named Abbey. Both were intrigued with Peggy Sue. Abbey was very protective of her and would sleep beneath the big cage keeping vigil over her new friend.

As Peggy Sue grew, she and I bonded and I learned how to handle her. She used to like to climb out of her cage and just sit on the top of it while I did my household chores. All my pets liked music, and Peggy Sue was no exception! I often left the radio on while at work so they'd have the sound of music to enjoy and keep them company. Peggy Sue would sit quietly atop her cage and when ready to go back inside could do so all by herself. She used her front legs to pull herself up the tree branch and into the hammock where she would fall asleep. Lisa had always told me squirrels just love hammocks and lots of rags and soft things to cuddle up in. If you offered them paper towels, they would shred them and soon make a nest. Peggy Sue's food bowl was always filled with fresh fruit, nuts, acorns in season and dandelions from my garden.

What an affectionate little squirrel she was! She would try and "groom" me, nibbling on my fingers and cleaning around my nails. Her little love bites never hurt as she was as gentle as could be with me. I cannot recall her ever hurting me whenever we interacted with each other.

I came to love Peggy Sue so very much, and the thought of losing her one day was devastating. I knew the chance of her surviving a long time with the injuries she'd sustained was slim. That dreaded time came on Easter, 1994. Only two years old, Peggy Sue's kidneys had begun to shut down. There was little my vet could do and she died that Easter Sunday. I never cried so hard. I'd been visiting my mother that day. We had a nice Easter dinner together. When I returned home I found my little friend had died. I was devastated. I'd become so attached to her that life without her seemed impossible. I still had Abbey my beloved Scottish terrier and Morris, the old marmalade kitty. I knew I had to carry on, they needed me too, and maybe someday Lisa would find me another squirrel that needed care. Lisa was kind and sympathetic when she heard the news. She told me what I already knew, that I'd done all I could and not to feel too badly. "There will be another one someday, don't be so sad, I often get calls from folks who find injured squirrels."

And so I buried Peggy in my back yard where I had buried so many others found hit in the road. That was hard enough, picking up those lifeless little bodies from the busy street, but laying little Peggy to rest was even harder. Returning to the house I stared at the big empty cage where she had spent so much of her time. I wanted to see it occupied again. Abbey and Morris sensed the loss too and tried their best to cheer me, but I knew there would never be another pet like that little squirrel, and I was determined to have another one in my care

Chapter Three

Here's Tommy

Over the next several months I continued playing with my outside buddies. I had lost a few of them too. Some simply disappeared which made me think the neighbors probably had a hand in that. They were constantly badgering me about the squirrels. I couldn't understand how city people who move to the suburbs would want to rid their yards of the wildlife there. They looked upon them all as "pests." My troubles with neighbors only worsened. A lot of rough characters were moving into the neighborhood bringing with them drugs and seedy friends. It was time to start thinking of selling and getting out, much as I hated to leave my backyard friends. It had been ten years, and I was tired of having to look over my shoulders every time I went out into my own yard. I'd taken a lot of abuse from the neighbors, and so had my squirrels.

One evening while I was readying myself to go out to dinner with a nice new gentleman friend, who should appear at my door but Lisa. She was carrying a cage with a small grey creature inside, not a squirrel....but a "chin"....

a grey chinchilla named Tommy. "Tommy's owner can no longer care for him" she said. "Would you like to have him?"

I wasn't terribly interested in having a chinchilla at the time, my heart was still missing my little Peggy and I'd so hoped to have another squirrel. Besides, I knew absolutely nothing about chinchillas! But Lisa insisted. She had all the instructions and books regarding their care and this little fellow needed a home. I knew Lisa had her hands full with so many baby squirrels and other creatures so how could I refuse?

"I guess I'll take him" I finally said, peering closer into the cage to get a better look. I'd never really seen a chinchilla before.

"He's awfully cute!" I said with a smile. And cute he was! Looking back now I probably scared off my date because after dinner when he dropped me off back home and drove off, I never heard from him again! I realized he most likely was no animal lover and the relationship would never have worked. "Well that's his tough luck" I said to Tommy. "Anyone who doesn't like animals isn't worth my time! Eventually I would have given him "the air" anyway!"

Tommy was great. It wasn't long before I began to really enjoy him and found myself buying toys and a wheel for him to run in. Eventually I bought him a bigger cage too. He loved balloons, and would reach up for the string and pull the balloon down towards him. He loved to stick his little nose up my nostril as a way of showing affection! Abbey and Morris got along so well with him. When Christmas time came, he got his special treats along with them. Tommy even had his own little Christmas tree which I set up in his room. He loved to look at the lights. Christmas was always a special holiday to me too and I would spend extra time making up peanut butter balls and cookies to string up on the trees outside for the squirrels and birds. I got such a kick out of seeing them go for those extra treats! Chestnuts, walnuts, pecans, hazelnuts.....all the very best for my little friends! Sure, I was spoiling them all, but I enjoyed it and obviously so did they. It lifted my spirits and made life all that much more pleasant, especially in light of the fact that I was surrounded by a bunch of those "other nuts."

Not long after Tommy came to live here my elderly cat Morris became sick. Morris was nearly 20 years old, a tough old boy who'd survived having the end of his tale bit off by my little Scottish terrier years before. I knew his health was failing because he was so thin. The dreaded day came when I had to make that decision to end his life and suffering. The vet agreed, his quality of life was not good. And so it was time to say goodbye to another dear friend.

Abbey was old too, going on thirteen years old. That's a good age for a Scotty, as they're not known for living much beyond the age of ten. Anything after that is considered a gift. I knew she missed Morris, they'd been buddies for many years. So now it was just Abbey, Tommy and me. I wondered if I would ever have another squirrel. I called Lisa often just to check if any others had come into her care but none had. She had plenty of healthy babies, but they would be released into the wild when old enough.

Still contemplating selling my house, I called a real estate agent and started the proceedings. I listed it with one realtor with little success. When the house had been on the market a long time, I listed with another.

While all this was going on with trying to sell the place, Lisa called with the great news.

"I think I have another squirrel for you!" she said. Just when I thought it would never happen again, and in the midst of trying to sell the house, suddenly the thought of leaving all my backyard friends made me so sad. I'd been so preoccupied with trying to get out of that neighborhood, sad to think of what would become of the squirrels and other wildlife, and now Lisa had found me another squirrel that needed care. Of course I was excited. I missed Peggy so much. It had been more than a year since I'd lost her. Apparently a woman who worked as a lineman for Bell Atlantic (or perhaps I should say line woman!) found a baby squirrel lying on the road beneath a telephone pole she was working on. She picked up the squirrel and placed it in the pocket of the flannel shirt she was wearing to keep it warm. Fortunately this woman had heard of Lisa and how she took care of injured and abandoned squirrels and she called her to see if she could bring it to her. Lisa asked me if I wanted to meet the woman and take the squirrel so she could check it over. I gladly went to meet the girl who was down near the shore and she handed me the tiny little grey creature. I held it close to me to keep it warm. I thanked the woman for finding it and drove back to Lisa's where she looked it over and informed me it was a female. Lisa reckoned it was only about six weeks old, possibly younger, so we fed it some formula. Its little eyes were open, and oh she was the sweetest little squirrel! I took her over to our vet and had her examined. Her injuries would mean she'd be paralyzed from the waist down for the rest of her life. Peggy Sue had had the same kind of injury, possibly from a fall. The vet assured me she was fine otherwise, but would never regain the use of her back legs. He looked at me and smiled.

"Looks like you'll be able to keep this one!" he said. Dr. Bell loved squirrels and he was an excellent vet. He'd taken care of all my pets in the past and I trusted his judgment. I was beaming with joy, happy to have another little squirrel to care for but sad at the same time to think of her injury. Another squirrel to call my own! I would name her Emily. My second pet squirrel......I was so happy! I left the vet's office with Emily that day and took her to her new home and placed her in the cage I had fixed up for her. That cage had been empty so long and Emily seemed very comfortable in the little hammock I placed inside for her. It was a new beginning for both of us and the start of a very special relationship that I would treasure the rest of my life.

Chapter Four

Emily

In the weeks that followed Emily adapted to her new home quickly and seemed quite content in the large cage that had been Peggy's home. She liked to snuggle up in the little fleece "blankies" I placed in there for her, pieces of larger blankets I no longer used. As she grew, she soon learned to climb the sturdy branch that reached up to her little hammock. It hung down in the center of the cage so she could see all around her from her lofty perch. It was there she would fall asleep at the end of each day, cuddle in her "blankies", surrounded by soft toys and stuffed animals I'd placed nearby. Emily played with them and amused herself while I was at work, and though handicapped and very young she maneuvered about the cage with great skill when not napping in her hammock.

Soon she was weaned from the formula I'd been giving her and with the arrival of autumn I was able to collect acorns for her. In addition to these I gave her walnuts, peanuts, hazelnuts, and various other nuts, her very favorite being pecans. It wasn't long before I was spoiling her with pecans every day. Her diet also included fresh veggies and fruit...apples, grapes, sweet potatoes, and raw corn off the cob. Several times each week I gave her vitamins, a liquid that she liked well enough to lap off my finger. My vet had recommended the vitamins to supplement her diet and help make her body strong.

My new little buddy and I were bonding well, doting on each other and enjoying each other's company. She was a joy to have around and I guess you could say I'd become her mother! Emily loved attention and so loved having her belly and chin rubbed she would just lie back and let me tickle her. While doing this I'd often see her extend her arms out and about her head, and she would stay in this amusing pose for a long while, enjoying each little rub and tickle. It became a ritual she looked forward to each day. Emily became so trusting that soon I could take her from the cage, let her sit atop my shoulder and walk about the house doing my chores while she went along for the ride. It was a contented time for both of us. Sometimes she would stretch out on my lap while I sat in my favorite chair, listening intently while I talked to her. She even liked watching T.V.! Often I'd catch her watching the screen from her hammock inside the cage, staring as if she understood what was going on. Emily had the uncanny ability to amuse herself and me too, slipping down from her hammock to play with her stuffed animals, poking holes in them at times or simply busying herself by burying her nuts! This she did with great care, packing them down neatly and covering them just so, always remembering where she'd buried her treasures. Even though she could not be in the wild, her natural instincts took over. It was the cutest thing to watch.

During this time I was still living in the townhouse and had Abbey the Scottish terrier and Tommy with me. The townhouse had been off the market for awhile but now with more trouble from neighbors rearing its ugly head I decided to try and sell it again. After listing it with a different realtor, I finally had it sold within 6 months. I needed to find a comfortable place for myself and my pets, someplace where I wouldn't feel threatened by neighbors each time I fed the squirrels and birds. I'd made so many animal friends and it broke my heart to think of leaving them behind, wondering if the new people who moved in would be kind to them.

A young woman bought my house. I explained my concern for the animals. How would they understand if suddenly their generous supply of peanuts and bird seed were no longer available too them? Though she seemed kind and promised to do her best to provide for the squirrels and birds, all I could do was pray the good Lord would look after them for me. After all, I'd spent day after day walking through the wooded area across the road with squirrels in tow and birds following overhead, scattering seeds and nuts for all to enjoy. It hurt to think of them looking for me, looking for the treats and the kind soul who'd provided them for so long. I wished I could take them all with me, but I knew this was not a logical thought. So it came to pass that I said my sad farewells to Frenchie, Himsey, Half Pint, Chips and so many others. My heart truly went out to them. Hopefully, the new owner would come to love and care for them as I had.

It was time to focus on my new home. I wanted a larger yard and privacy from neighbors. While this house searching went on and my life was in transition, Abbey suddenly took ill. She stopped eating and became very lethargic. One morning, she simply wouldn't get up. A trip to the vet brought grave news.....Abbey's kidneys were failing. She was old. She had to be euthanized. This devastating news couldn't have come at a worse time. I

was reeling with the thought of having to deal with the loss of another pet so soon. Yet deal with it I must. Abbey was thirteen years old when she passed away. I had no place to bury her because now I was in the process of moving. I had no choice but to leave her with the vet to be cremated. Abbey was a delightful dog. She got along with everyone, including other animals, and everyone loved her too. My heart was breaking when I left her, and to this day I've never been able to replace her in my home or my heart. My years with Abbey had led to a large collection of Scotty dog memorabilia.....everything from vintage toys and rugs to paintings and figurines..... a million Scotty things, all reminders of my beloved pet. She had been the second Scottish terrier in my life, and she would be greatly missed.

With Abbey gone the house was very quite, just me, Emily and my nocturnal friend Tommy. While I was working Emily had no one to interact with. I sensed how much she missed Abbey lying beneath her cage during the day. Abbey had been good company for Emily. I'd been packing things up for the big move and boxes were everywhere now. How I hated moving, and hoped this would be the last move for a very long time. I just longed to be settled someplace at last.

Chapter Five

The Big Move

I finally settled on a cute little bungalow in Deptford, New Jersey, only about ten miles from where I had been living. Much smaller than the townhouse, it had but one floor and that would take some getting used to. Luckily this house had a nice basement for storage and a wonderful, large back yard. The yard was surrounded by woods and it wasn't long before the birds and squirrels found me once more, checking me out and delighting in the nuts and seeds I offered. Off the kitchen was a nice large deck and the squirrels soon found their way up to it where they sat eating their peanuts. While Emily and Tommy were adjusting to their new surroundings, I was busy getting acquainted with the neighborhood and making the place homey. My knack for decorating came in handy as I turned the little heated sun porch at the front of the house into a dining area. The previous owners had left an old upright piano behind, a rather nice addition to the place which I decided to have properly tuned once I got settled in. I made the bungalow a cozy place, and Emily loved going out on the deck to watch the other animals. I took her outside with me, holding her close as she clung to me. She never tried to run away, she just enjoyed watching the other animals with great curiosity.

One morning I found that the house next door, which had been empty a long time, suddenly had new occupants. They were renters, young teenagers who didn't take long to start annoying everyone around them. I couldn't believe it! Was I going to have trouble with neighbors again? Each night brought waves of loud music from their open windows, yelling, partying, and generally carrying on till all hours. Not only could I not sleep, my pets couldn't either! It was useless calling the police, they did nothing. I mustered my courage and tried talking to the offending neighbors, but that was a waste of time. Other neighbors were also complaining, but nothing was ever done. Eventually I decided I'd have to move yet again, and the thought of boxing up all my possessions and up-rooting myself and my pets in such a short time was unbearable. But I was not going to live in that environment, upsetting myself and my pets as well, and since no one seemed inclined to do anything about the disgusting neighbors, I had little choice but to leave. Once again my property went up for sale.

It was early in February when I got up one morning and went into Tommy the chinchilla's room as I always did to feed him. He lay there motionless on his cage floor. He wouldn't move. Though it was a bitter cold day I knew I had to rush him to the vet. But when I went out to my car, someone had slashed a tire. No doubt one of the rowdy neighbors had done this to me. They never cared for me because I had asked them time and time again to tone down their loud noise so I could get some sleep! In despair I ran across the street to the one neighbor who was friendly and caring. She adored animals and didn't hesitate to lend me her car so I could transport Tommy to the vet. To make matters worse, it was snowing that day. I wrapped Tommy in a blanket and held him close on my lap as I rushed to the animal hospital. Moments after I arrived, he died. Though the vet could find no cause for his sudden demise, a sudden seizure or stroke could not be ruled out. Tommy was only eight or nine years old, and "chins" (chinchillas) often live to be fifteen. With all the turmoil in my life I found myself with a broken heart once more. I was weary from the heart aches and dissatisfaction with my new surroundings, the terrible neighbors and the thought of moving again.I knew I couldn't bury Tommy at this place, so I called upon Lisa once again. Lisa was only too happy to allow me to bury him in her back yard. She had had many pets of her own buried there. Tommy would rest in a beautiful garden there, a garden Lisa's son took great care with. Lisa's husband kindly prepared a place for Tommy, and that is where he rests now. There's a marker with his name and a statue of St. Francis too. It's been so long ago now, but I know I can visit there whenever I want. I knew I was always welcome at Lisa's. It felt right placing Tommy there, as Lisa was the one who'd given him to me.

My little family was dwindling. It was just Emily and I now. She spent her days alone, without Tommy to keep her company. For even though he slept most of the day, I always wheeled his cage into Emily's room before going to work so he could be with her and she could see him and know another animal friend was there. She had gotten used to that, and now she would be alone. To help compensate for this, I gave Emily a lot of extra attention when I was home. We both missed Tommy very much. In his own way, he too was a very lovable creature. I began to wonder if I would ever find that peaceful place I'd been searching so long for.

Chapter Six

Apartment Life

In time I sold the little bungalow and moved into an apartment. I was still in the same general area, and for the time being it seemed the best thing for me and Emily. I wasn't ready to buy a house yet, I just wanted to wait until the right place came along. So I bided my time and made do with the one bedroom apartment, selling off a lot of things to make room and putting others in storage. It would be the best thing to do for awhile. The apartment was plenty big for me and Emily. We were on the second floor with a balcony and big sliding glass doors with a nice view overlooking a courtyard and park-like setting. I placed Emily's cage right by the door where she could look outside and get lots of sun. As you can imagine, it wasn't long before I had the local squirrels climbing up onto the balcony where I put peanuts out each day. Emily seemed to get a kick out of watching them too. What little rascals they were! Watching them kept her amused and they too were curious about her. I had to be careful though. One day when the nice weather allowed me to open the sliding doors for Emily,   a squirrel managed to chew a large hole in the screen. I hadn't been watching and that squirrel might've tried to attack Emily through her cage.

Fortunately this time I had pleasant neighbors at the apartment complex. The lady downstairs was especially friendly. For her, having a friend with a pet squirrel was a unique experience. It was my plan to stick out apartment living for at least a year as I missed having a place of my own but wanted to take enough time to search for a nice place. It was during my stay at the apartment that Emily developed a bad habit....she started chewing her feet. At first I thought she was nervous about her new accommodations. I called my old friend Lisa who told me that squirrels sometimes do this, and might even chew badly enough in the wild as to lose a foot or limb. To avoid this "self mutilation" I went to the health food store and purchased some Tea Tree oil. Despite the horrible smell, the oil is good for healing wounds and the smell alone would surely keep Emily from chewing herself. Eventually it worked and she was looking much better. Unfortunately I had to keep applying the oil, what a mess! If I stopped for a few days she went right back to chewing. I hated to see her doing this to herself, and felt so helpless. I had to get more creative with my treatments. An antiseptic solution from the vet was used to clean her feet. My vet thought Emily had a behavioral problem. I decided to cut some old gloves and slip the "fingers" over her feet, then I wrapped a bandage around that and dabbed a bit of Tea Tree oil on the cloth. Emily had homemade booties and she looked so funny! She continued to wear those little booties for a long time but they kept her from chewing her feet and that was all that mattered. It took a lot of hard work and dedication to this little squirrel but I utterly loved her and wouldn't trade my life with her for anything. It was unconditional love on both our parts. I admit at times I became very frustrated, but it was only because I felt inadequate in my ability to do more for Emily. Never once did I regret taking her in and caring for her. That is what I wanted to do and she was well worth all the sacrifices. I had known only one other person in my life who had squirrels as pets and that was Lisa. I truly felt having Emily was a once in a life time experience and I was grateful for it.

The chewing problem persisted over the next few months so I decided to have my vet, Dr. Bell, look at her. Dr. Bell was so good with squirrels and little Emily was always on her best behavior. I had no way of knowing what was bothering Emily, perhaps she had a severe skin itch, or mites, even her ears kept bothering her. But Dr. Bell couldn't find anything unusual other than she might have a behavioral problem of unknown origin. Emily seemed perfectly happy, always affectionate with me and very appreciative of the attention I gave her. I started giving her even more attention, and after a while she seemed to calm down and stopped the biting. Eventually she was so much better I was able to remove the booties.

Chapter Seven

The New Home (House #3)

I was now in a position financially to look for another home for me and Emily. Right around the corner from where we'd been living in the apartment was a cute little rancher with a nice sized yard. It also had a deck off the back bedroom. Situated on a little hill, the house was surrounded by wooded lots. After some thought I decided to buy the house and Emily and I moved in. It was perfect timing. Spring was around the corner and before long I had all the neighborhood birds and squirrels at my door once again. It seemed no matter where I lived, I always had the animals quite literally eating out of my hand! I set up my birdfeeders and a very nice neighbor behind me made me a nice feeder which I thought was very special. He was one of the nicest people, offering to keep my grass cut and help with the yard work I couldn't do. He had quite a knack for gardening and soon had the place looking beautiful. There was a nice Polish family across the street and the woman there was very knowledgeable on flowers. She was so kind, transplanting all sorts of flowers from her garden into mine. I had a cute little house and it was beginning to feel like this might be it, no more moves for me. Finally, I had a place to settle down and call home. Emily was the talk of the town and the neighbors who knew her just loved her. She picked up on which neighbors were my friends and she was always willing to let them pet her or give her a scratch on the neck. Emily stayed in the living room where she could look out the great big window. She had plenty of sunshine and fresh air on nice days. I loved how she would lie in her hammock and enjoy a warm summer breeze. Sometimes I would take a little nap with her on the couch next to her cage. A couple of friendly outside squirrels would often make their way up on the deck and would peek in my front door when it was open. At that time I had a full view glass storm door and they could see in and Emily and I could look out. I had befriended one little fellow who would come in if you opened the door. That seemed to amuse Emily! He would creep in and look around as if to say, "I wouldn't mind living here myself, it's so nice and cozy!" Emily and the other squirrels would sometimes gaze at each other curiously. Often I wondered if she had the longing to be outdoors with the other squirrels. At times I felt so bad for her and wished she could have lived the life she was meant to, climbing trees, having babies, being mischievous when the urge struck. Fate had dealt her a blow with her affliction, but I was able to give her a life. God must have put Emily in my life for a reason. It certainly gave my life purpose. She gave me more love and joy than anyone could imagine. Only if you've had the pleasure of living life with a squirrel can you understand how I feel! In my heart I felt we had a bond that would last an eternity. We doted on each other, Emily and I. You could say I had become her mother, or at least the only mother she had ever known. The longer she lived with me, the more attached we became to each other and the stronger the bond became. I knew it would be hard to say goodbye someday, as well I knew I must. The bond only strengthened. We were inseparable!

Perhaps it was out of boredom that Emily continued to chew and bite her feet. The creative booties I'd made from old gloves were a necessity most of the time otherwise she would do great damage to herself. She loved to play, and her cage was now her playground with stuffed animals, wooden blocks to chew and other toys. Squirrels must chew to prevent their teeth from getting too long. Emily loved her toys! Once in awhile, when in a particularly playful mood, we both would wrestle with those stuffed animals and play tug of war. Often I found her curled up with one, sound asleep. Sometimes I found nuts and food buried inside the stuffed toys. She made holes in her blankets too. It was pointless to try and keep her cage tidy for Emily had a way of rearranging her décor to suit her own needs! Once in a while she'd growl or hiss at me as if to say, "Don't touch that! This is my stuff!"

The cage that Emily called home was large and roomy. I'd had it custom made so she would have plenty of room to move around. Lisa's son Richie had added plexi-glass halfway around the inside so Emily could climb up without getting her feet caught in the one inch metal openings. Lisa had told me how squirrels could injure their feet on the metal and Emily had enough problems with her feet. The plexi-glass prevented her from grabbing onto any of the openings that might cause her to get caught or hurt. This was especially important since I was away at work all day and wanted to insure her safety. The bottom floor of the cage was flat metal and I placed soft fleece blankets there for her to scoot around and play in without getting tied up in any threads. Fleece is wonderful as it doesn't thread and is very soft. Before I came to use it Emily had tangled herself in some threads, nearly cutting off the circulation to her leg. She could've died had I not discovered it and removed it in time. Her hammock was also fashioned of fleece, hanging down from the top of the cage held up by little wire hooks. Lisa had given me a long branch to place inside so Emily could move up and down with ease. She would curl up in a ball and cover herself with her blanket. This was the time I loved to scratch her belly or tickle her under her chin. Emily loved it! She would gently take my fingers and nibble them ever so slightly, her way of showing affection. Sometimes she bit down a little too hard, but it was out of love, not anger. "Kisses, kisses!" I would say to her before going to bed. "Sleep tight Emily, mommy loves you!"

Then I'd go off to bed too, knowing she was safe and secure. Come morning, Emily was given fresh water, plenty of fresh fruits, veggies and nuts. She always got some pecans before I left for work, a special treat! They were her favorite. When acorns were plentiful in fall she got them too and my sister Chris would often gather nice big fat ones from her home in New Hampshire and send them by post. Dandelions in spring and acorns in fall were some of Emily's favorite foods. It was easy to gather plenty of dandelions from my yard for her. Around Christmas time, chestnuts were a big hit with Emily as well as my outside buddies who shared in the holiday treat.

Life in Blackwood wasn't too bad. I'd made a couple of friends in the neighborhood and things seemed to be going ok until one day the people who lived next door to me decided to get two police dogs. The man worked for the police department and seemed nice at first but when they transferred him to the Canine Unit he had to take these two huge dogs home with him. They were

 left outside 24 hours a day. He never brought them in and they barked incessantly, depriving me of sleep and likely upsetting Emily too. I tried talking to the neighbors, but it did no good. He was well liked in the police department and taking him to court for disturbing my peace was not an option. When he heard I was considering that, he threatened to have Emily taken away and destroyed. According to him it was against the law to have a wild

animal living in your home. I began to feel more and more intimidated by his threats and was getting sick for lack of sleep. Other neighbors were upset too by his barking dogs but no one seemed inclined to try and do anything about it.

I decided I had to do something or I'd lose my mind! I had no where else to go and no one to turn to, so I called on an old boyfriend I had dated for a short time years before. After explaining my situation to him I told him I needed a place to hide Emily. Naturally he was very surprised to hear from me but offered to let me and Emily stay with him until I could figure out what I wanted to do. I began to harbor thoughts of getting back together with him, getting away from the neighbors and selling my house once more.

So Emily and I moved in with him. Most of my possessions remained in Blackwood so I just took what I needed to make Emily and myself comfortable. But it wasn't a good move, and before a week had passed the situation turned ugly. I knew it wasn't going to work out. There I was at a dead end again not knowing which way to turn for help. I couldn't bear the thought of going back to my house and the unpleasant confrontation with the neighbors that was sure to follow. In desperation I called my friend Lisa and told her my dilemma. Lisa had a house she was renting but the people had gone months before and it was empty. She and her husband had been fixing it up, but it was perfectly livable. If I could manage to sell my house I could move in and pay Lisa rent until I decided what I wanted to do. What a dear friend I had in her, she was so understanding! I put my home in Blackwood up for sale and it sold quickly. In the meantime, I rented the house from Lisa in Westmont, New Jersey. It was a small 1930's cottage on a dead-end street, in need of work but quite cozy. God knows Emily and I were so tired of moving from place to place! I just wanted a place to stay put. This seemed the ideal spot to settle down.

Chapter Eight

The Cottage in the Woods

The small cottage that had meant so much to Lisa and Dick was shaping up and beginning to feel more like a real home. There was a large yard and a clear running brook that backed up to the bottom of the hill behind my lot. Huge trees including beautiful oaks and maples afforded shade and privacy. It was a nature lover's dream in the midst of the New Jersey metropolis. Though Lisa had had work done before I moved in previous renters had done considerable damage so I began the task of repairing the most important things and replacing the windows using savings I'd tucked away. I applied for a no-interest loan offered by the county and was approved allowing more upgrades to the place without draining all my savings. The house and little garage were painted and a flagstone path to the front door put down. Eventually I would run a fence along the front of the property with a gate across the driveway. Located on a dead-end street, there seemed to be ample privacy. In the early morning hours all you heard were birds singing! On warm summer nights the gentle breezes blew the curtains and I heard the outside creatures stirring. There seemed to be an abundance of wildlife including raccoons, possums, and of course...

squirrels! There was even a woodchuck I named "Chucky Cheese." He loved apples and peaches. Lisa and Dick had rehabilitated a woodchuck they named Heidi. Heidi was so tame she slept under the covers with Dick. Eventually they had to release her into the wild. She adjusted very well to her natural environment but often returned to visit Lisa and Dick.

It didn't take long for all the squirrels and birds to learn that they could get a good hand-out from me and soon I had squirrels coming in the tens and twenties! Word soon gets around in the animal kingdom and soon their families and friends were visiting too in search of the goodies I offered.

Emily and I grew very close during my first few years in the cottage. She loved it there. I placed her big cage by a sunny window in the living room next to the couch so she could be close to me when I relaxed and watched television. On nice days I opened the windows and she could feel the breeze. The house had a nice sun porch off the kitchen too and many times Emily and I would sit out there and watch the other squirrels, chipmunks and birds scurrying around in search of nuts and seeds. It was a great place to sit and relax with a pleasant view for us both. I'd had it freshly painted and decorated with white wicker furniture and a little fountain. Pictures adorned the walls and new carpeting made it comfy. Often Emily would sit atop my shoulder while I sipped a cup of tea there. It was so important to me that both of us finally have some peace and a nice place to live and for the most part we did. The next door neighbors were a nice quiet couple who also loved nature and animals. They were wonderful gardeners and the woman helped me get some of my own gardens started. Emily fascinated them! They always had a kind word and scratch on the head for her when I was outside with Emily on my shoulder. In time I had beautiful roses, azaleas, hostas, lavender and lilies...Lisa's favorite flower. Little Emily and I both loved walking around the house admiring the gardens and enjoying the sunshine. She was so content to stay in my arms, sometimes stretching out on my lap for a long nap. Other squirrels I'd befriended would come close to check her out but Emily would just give them a curious look and go back to sleep. This was the most peaceful time I had with her. I valued those moments more than anything.

As time passed and she grew older, Emily became more loveable and content. She didn't seem so anxious and nervous anymore. The biting had all but stopped. Of course, being handicapped as she was, Emily depended on me for everything.

There were some close calls with her health, and the time she became so lethargic for no reason at all. But I remembered Lisa telling me that during mating season or when females come "into heat" they sometimes become depressed. I began giving her vitamins and hand feeding her in hopes of alleviating the condition. The extra attention brought her around but it made me aware of the fact that someday I would lose her too, and I had to face that. For now things were back to normal, at least as "normal" as they could be, for in my life nothing ever seemed normal!

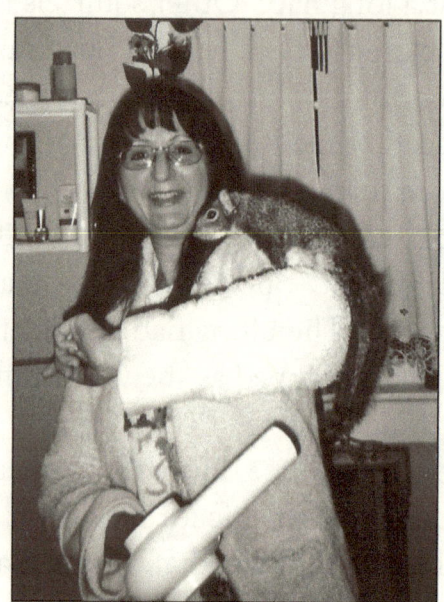

Emily awaits her coiffure!

Chapter Nine

Bath Time for Emily

Weekends were Emily's bath time and also the time for cleaning her cage.   Believe it or not, this little gal *loved* her bath which consisted of applying a little soap and warm water around her back-side and tail, the areas she could not clean herself. Then a warm rinse-off under the faucet, towel drying and a more thorough dry with my hair blow-dryer! While this might frighten some pets, Emily loved it and sat up on my lap while I was blow drying her. What a sight to behold! Never once did she try to bite or scratch me. She even enjoyed being combed afterward. She had the best disposition I'd ever seen in a squirrel. Possibly she was simply grateful someone was caring for her so well.

I brushed and fluffed her tail and I do believe she knew how spiffy she looked when I was done. All the fussing and primping made her feel better! Back into her clean cage I would place her and she'd pull herself up into her little hammock and go to sleep.

On Sunday mornings when I could sleep in longer I would take Emily out of her cage, take her out of her hammock and bring her into bed under the covers with me. It was my favorite time with her.

Mornings were peaceful, nothing to bother us but the sound of the birds outside my bedroom window. Emily looked so content curled up next to me with her paw covering one eye. Sometimes she'd lie across my chest or go up above my head on the pillow, stretch out and lie down. As I stroked her gently she would fall asleep. Then I'd whisper softly and tell her how much she meant to me and how special she was. It made me so happy to feel her trust in me as I held her in my arms. You just can't put a price on something like that.

Weekends were the only times I could slow down and relax with Emily. I hated being away from her five days a week. Sometimes I'd rush home at lunch just to check on her. She was always happy to see me and I would take her out of her cage and bring her into the sunroom or out into the yard. She loved the warm sun on her body. From the safety of the kitchen window she would watch the other squirrels. Sometimes one would perch atop the gas grill and look at us through the kitchen window. Other times they'd put on a show for us, jumping and playing with each other. They were quite the clowns, and I could write stories about their antics too! When it was time to return to work I'd give Emily a kiss and hug and place her back in her hammock where she'd sleep most of the day till I came home again. Emily managed to keep herself amused, playing with the toys I'd put in her cage and chewing on her wooden blocks. She could demolish a block of wood in no time, splintering it into a million pieces! In the evenings when I sat watching T.V. with my hands in my lap, Emily would sit on my lap with her paws folded around mine. I felt so much love from that little squirrel. To have a relationship like that with a wild creature was truly special and unique, and I don't think words can convey just how good it made me feel. Caring for Emily was a commitment I was glad to make, even though it meant sacrificing vacations. It was hard to find someone as committed to her care if I went away. My sister was living in New England during these years and often I wanted to visit her, but it was just too difficult to find someone to care for a squirrel and a chinchilla! This was not your usual pet-sitting job and it required having someone trustworthy and caring stay overnight. But Emily was definitely worth the sacrifice of vacations. Bath time, Sunday mornings and other quality time after work were all moments I treasured with Emily.

Chapter Ten

The Photographer

For a long time I had wanted to get professional photos done of Emily so I'd have them to remember her by after she was gone. I found Marr Bailey, a professional photographer who came to the house one day to "see his subject." He was excited at the prospect of photographing a squirrel.

"I've photographed a lot of people and their pets" he said, "but never a pet squirrel!" This would be a real challenge for him and a welcome change from the usual wedding shots. Much to our surprise, Emily wasn't camera shy. Though I'd photographed her and some of her outside buddies with a cheap camera I wanted some nice professional close-ups. Getting Emily ready for her "photo shoot" was fun. She seemed to perk up as Marr went to work setting up the tripod and extra lighting in the living room where I sat with her on my lap. Emily was indeed "ready for her close-up" as she looked straight into the camera much to the delight of both the photographer and myself! Then we moved into the kitchen where the wonderful lighting resulted in some really beautiful shots of her sitting on my shoulder.

Marr put together a wonderful photo album of Emily and me with some photos in color and some in beautiful sepia tones. I was very happy with his work and I do believe Emily was too! She had a great time and I think Marr came away from the photo session with experiences he'd never forget. Emily had been quite the little ham and I now have a house full of beautiful photos of her.

The Christmas that followed found me buying a nice camera for my sister Chris who had shown an interest in learning photography herself. When she visited from New Hampshire she, too, took some lovely photos of me and Emily which I framed and placed in albums. I have many wonderful memories of my little friend that I treasure. I love showing them off to people as they're not the sort of photos you see everyday. Marr Bailey has since left the area and moved elsewhere. If ever I locate him again and he gets a copy of this story I'll thank him once more for his time and efforts to capture Emily as she truly was, a gentle, loving and very personable creature who came into my life through God's grace.

Chapter Eleven

What's It All About, Alfie?"

Emily had already outlived Abbey, Morris, Tommy and a couple of mice, all former pets. Despite her disabilities it was truly amazing how long she hung on. She was a strong gal who loved me and her life with me. One day I received a call from a friend who raised chinchillas. Hilda told me that one of her baby "chins" had a mishap resulting in a broken hind leg. It wasn't mendable and the leg would have to be amputated. Of course that meant she could never sell him. She asked if I would consider taking him on as another pet. At first I was very hesitant because for so long it had just been me and Emily. I had had chinchillas before (Tommy) and perhaps Emily would like the company. Another "heartbeat" in the house might be good for us both.

I named the newcomer "Alfie" and set to work acclamating him to his new surroundings. Emily seemed quite amused by him. She and Tommy had been good friends and she missed him when he passed away. So it was that Emily and Alfie too became friends and she seemed to enjoy the company. I felt a bit relieved knowing she'd have another creature in the house while I was away at work. Alfie was a cutie pie. He was all white with a big grey patch on his butt and some grey areas around his head. Being a young chinchilla, he was afraid to be alone at night when I first took him in. And because chins are nocturnal, he kept me up all night! The little guy wanted to be entertained all night and I needed my sleep! With a wheel to spin around in and his jumping to and fro he made quite the racket all night. Eventually I found that leaving a radio on helped quiet him down. He was very lovable and Emily liked having him around. Every day I brought him out into the living room to spend time with us until it was bedtime. Then it was off to sleep for me and Emily and little Alfie became the "night watchman." I was glad I'd taken him in because I knew if something happened to Emily at least I would not be alone again without an animal to care for. Over the years I'd befriended many outside creatures and taken in some of them only to have my heart broken when they died. But death is part of life. Having another pet would at least soften the blow when Emily was gone. Living alone as I do with family and friends far away, it's such a comfort having a pet.

Chapter Twelve

Lisa's Illness

Lisa and Dick Bakely were very good friends. I had
known Lisa a long time. She taught me all I know
about the raising and caring of squirrels and had herself
rehabilitated hundreds. People from all over knew of her.
They knew if they found a sick or injured animal she was
the one to take it to. Lisa had been battling leukemia
and kidney disease for a while now. She also had diabetes
and eventually had to go on dialysis. I remember visiting
her a couple of times in the hospital while she was having
dialysis treatment and it was very hard seeing her like
that. I worried that she might not make it much longer
and I would feel lost without her. We'd had such good
times together in the past. I wanted her to get well and be
around many more years.

One day I went to visit her in a rehab facility. She
had taken a bad fall after being home for a short time and
had to be returned to this place where she could be cared
for. Dick was having health issues too and felt she would
get the care she needed there. The last time I saw Lisa she
looked great and said she was feeling well enough to go
home. That was good news to hear. I was anxious to have

her over to see Emily and all the new things I was doing
to the house and yard. Lisa had always loved this house
and grounds. She always praised my efforts at fixing it up,
planting the gardens and of course, caring for Emily. I was
home one evening when the phone rang and it was Dick.
Lisa had slipped into a coma after having a severe stroke. I
was devastated by the news. I couldn't bear losing my dear
friend.

I visited Lisa as often as I could and tried to have some
private time with her. I remember sitting at her bedside,
not knowing if she could hear me or even knew I was
there, telling her how much I loved her and how grateful
I was that I'd met her. I would sit and tell her too how
thankful I was for Emily and the knowledge of squirrels
she had passed on to me. Lisa remained in a coma for ten
days. A tough German, hard-headed and stubborn, I was
sure she'd pull through and be alright. But that was not
to be. Lisa died shortly after and I was devastated. I miss
her to this day and will always remember her and what she
taught me. Four years have passed since she died, but she
left me with so much.

Just a year before Lisa died my mother had passed
away too after a battle with lung cancer that spread to her
bones and eventually her brain. The surgery she'd had
on her legs only hastened her end. Sis and I both felt that
was a huge mistake, but her husband thought otherwise.
Losing both her and Lisa in just a little over a year was an
enormous drain on me emotionally and physically. With
the arrival of the 21st century it seemed I was hit with so
much heartache. Living by myself and having to cope

with the emotional upheavals was difficult for me, but my pets certainly helped soften the blow. They were always a comfort to me. For sis and me, the family has dwindled to just a few cousins living far away in Florida. Though we live in different parts of the country we're very close and have a lot in common. We both love music and art, and I've relied on her talents to help with Emily's story. In the past Chris wrote articles for two national herb magazines. She always loved dabbling in poetry and drawing too. Helping me with this book has been a new challenge with her busy schedule and I'm thankful for her help. I pray she and I and our few remaining family members in Florida stay healthy, love and cherish each other and above all stay in touch during the remaining years God grants to us.

Chapter Thirteen

Thanksgiving and A Holiday Scare

Hilda had given me Alfie the chinchilla around Thanksgiving and it was now going on a year since he joined me and Emily. Thanksgiving was upon us once again. The holidays were always a special time for family and friends and it was also a time to give a little extra something to my furry buddies. Alfie and Emily always got their favorite treats as did the animals outside. But with the passing of my mom and Lisa, this could not be as happy a holiday as it should've been. I missed them so much and with sis in New Hampshire visits were not easy. I had managed to spend one Thanksgiving and Christmas with her and enjoyed being in New England at that time of year. Fall is a beautiful time of year to be in that part of the country, though I recall having some difficulties with traveling that time. I had found a pet sitter, a challenge in itself, and my pets were well cared for. They were very happy to see me though when I returned. While it was good to get away for a few days I missed them too, and all the outside "buddies." I made my special Christmas cookies, punched holes in them and hung them outside on trees for the animals to enjoy. I also gathered pine cones, spread them with peanut butter and rolled them in birdseed. They all "went nuts" over the treat! Then I spread mixed nuts and sunflower seeds for all the birds and squirrels to enjoy. Emily and I would watch from the kitchen window as they came to take their Christmas treats. Inside, Alfie and Emily both got Christmas stockings filled with treats and their cages decorated too. There were banana chips, hazelnuts and apple pellets for Alfie and chestnuts, pecans and acorns from New Hampshire for Emily. She especially loved her pecans and the nice plump acorns sis would send by post. Each got a plush new toy to play and cuddle with. Emily would chew holes in hers and hide her nuts inside. I found many a nut carefully "squirreled" away inside her toys! She loved strutting about her cage with that stocking in her mouth, reaching inside for a choice pecan or chestnut. And woe to me if I tried to go near it! She was very possessive of her Christmas stocking! Nearing eleven years of age, Emily was getting up in "squirrel years." She seemed to require even more of my time now and somehow I knew my time with her was getting short.

Holidays came and went as they always do, another new year with new beginnings and hopefully a brighter future. Unfortunately, the year would bring about an end to some things too. Early in the new year Emily began biting at her feet again. For some unknown reason this behavior kept getting worse. I decided to take her to a different vet, one who was familiar with exotic animals and with this problem in particular. It seemed another opinion was in order. Emily was very good whenever I had to take her to the vet. From checkups to having her teeth clipped, she was always well behaved and the staff loved her. I wanted to get to the bottom of this self-abuse problem she suffered from. In the past, tests revealed no problems with parasites, ear infections or anything else. The new vet suggested putting her under anesthesia and looking deeper to see if there was a small tumor. There's always a risk at putting small wild creatures like Emily under anesthesia and I was apprehensive about it. But I had to take a chance in order to finally solve the problem of her constant chewing. So I gave my consent and sat in the waiting room anxiously awaiting the diagnosis. When I was told the anesthesia had to be interrupted because Emily's heart had stopped for a second or two and they had to revive her I was panicked. The vet said she would be alright, so I took her home and she slept the rest of the day.

I went about my usual routine for the rest of that afternoon. It was Saturday and I had a lot of household chores to keep me busy. Emily hadn't eaten all day and I was worried about her. At dinnertime I noticed she'd come down from her hammock and was spinning in circles in an uncontrollable way that really frightened me. A call to the vet relieved my mind somewhat as they said it was likely the anesthesia wearing off and that I should just give it time. But it took a couple of days before Emily was back to her self again. She was eating and drinking as usual and that seemed like a good sign. I was determined never to put her through that ordeal ever again. The vet couldn't tell me why she was chewing her feet so badly and I felt the anesthesia had done far more harm than good. Emily had been through a lot in her lifetime and perhaps the paralysis made her chew. Not knowing the circumstances under which she became paralyzed I knew it was also possible her traumatic experience had brought about neurological problems as well. All I knew was that Emily was my best buddy and I didn't want to lose her.

Chapter Fourteen

Summer of 2006-Darkening Shadows

Eleven years is a long life for a squirrel. Though
some live longer in captivity Emily's injuries made that
unlikely. I now considered each day with her a gift as her
life expectancy grew shorter. We celebrated her eleventh
birthday on the same day as my own birthday (August 1ˢᵗ)
each year. She looked like an "August baby" so I made
my special day hers too. This August, however, would be
different. For some reason I felt she would be sharing
her last birthday with me this year. Since that trip to the
vet, she hadn't been the same. In March of that year she
began losing weight. I noticed her bumping into things
inside her cage and having difficulty finding her food and
water bowls. It hurt me so much to see her this way. I
wanted to be with her every minute and now I had to
help her eat and drink. It was even harder now to be
away at work seven or eight hours a day. I worried every
second I was away. I did everything possible to make her
comfortable and place food and water within easy reach.
The water was the tough part. Emily had trouble making
her way around the cage and she stopped using the water
bottle which hung inside. The water bowl I left on her

blankets often got knocked over, wetting her bedding and her as well. Though I knew I was doing all I could for her, it frustrated me that I couldn't do more. I felt anger that something like this should happen to my faithful companion of eleven years. I never wanted to see her have to suffer again. I would have gladly taken her suffering instead. Despite all I did I knew I was losing another dear friend. I didn't want to see her like this but I couldn't have her euthanized either, so I just continued to do all I could to make her comfortable and gave her as much attention and love as I could. Whenever I was home I fed her on my lap and used an eyedropper to make sure she had water. I started giving her more Nutrical vitamins too. She loved the taste and it provided her with much needed nutrition. Leaving Emily during the work week had become so difficult I started bringing her to work with me. In this way I could make sure she had enough food and water. What a little trooper she was! I placed her in a large plastic container, the kind you use to store blankets and clothes. Her own blankets and toys went inside and I kept her on the desk behind mine. Since there is no one but me in the back office the few people I work with weren't bothered by her presence. She slept all day while I worked and it made me feel a lot better having her with me. Now Emily would have all the food and water she needed, but despite my efforts I knew what the outcome would be. You always pray and hope for a miracle and sometimes you get one. Emily had always been a little miracle to me from day one and she had made it through some tough times. It was now time for her to be at peace. She was getting old, and like humans the day comes when you just can't hold on any longer. The body gives out, even if the spirit is still willing. The time to say farewell was at hand. I always told Emily while holding her close that one day she would go to sleep and when she awoke she would see Aunt Lisa, grandmom, Abbey, Morris, Tommy and all the creatures that had lived with us before and she would be able to run and climb trees in a beautiful garden where no harm would ever come to her. Never again would she feel pain or suffer. She would be the squirrel she was created to be, free and able to live the normal life she'd been cheated of. But something good had come of her handicap. Emily's disabilities had enabled me to have a precious gift at a time in my life when I had already lost one squirrel I dearly loved and I needed to fill the big void in my life. And I had so enjoyed taking care of her. I gave up a lot but she was more than worth it! People think I'm crazy but that's o.k. I feel fortunate to have had that special closeness and bonding Emily and I shared. It was a once-in-a-lifetime experience that only a true animal lover would appreciate.

I used to say to Emily, "One day when mommy's time is over on this earth and I close my eyes for the last time I will wake up on the other side where family and friends will be waiting to greet me...and there you will be... running towards me! You'll climb up on me and lay in my arms once again. We will be together again some day " I would promise her as I continued to watch her fade.

Chapter Fifteen

Letting Go

The days were now growing shorter and shorter for Emily and me. I knew that soon I'd lose her. Each morning before leaving for work I tried giving her food and water, as much as she would take. It was hard now for her to eat her favorite nuts so I started using peanut butter, cashew butter and almond butter, spoon feeding her or letting her lick from my fingers. I gave her applesauce, pureed carrots, and sweet potatoes. All the foods she loved now had to be softened and mashed up. Peanut butter and mashed up fruit and veggies were left inside her cage where she could find them while I was at work. Emily continued to weaken despite my efforts and it became increasingly more difficult for her to move around her cage. No matter how much I fed her, she continued to fail. I spent all my free time caring for her now. I didn't want to do anything or go any where, I just wanted to be with her. I held her more now and talked to her all the time. Emily loved snoozing next to me. It was our little ritual each Sunday morning before she'd taken sick and she loved it. Sunday's were lazy days for us. I didn't have to rush off to work and we could sleep in. I loved the way she would sometimes lay across my chest or up above my head, her little eyes part-way closed. She had such a sweet face and was always so gentle around me. How would I be able to live without her?

I thought about the way she'd sit on my lap with her paws curled around my hands. The old pink rocking chair was her favorite place to sit with me. Sometimes I'd give her one of her toys to chew and in no time she'd have it splintered in pieces. She wasn't doing that anymore. Most of the time all she did was sleep. The old fight wasn't in her anymore and she started eating less. As much as I dreaded it I had to prepare myself for a life without Emily. My heart was heavy. I felt so frustrated and helpless because there was nothing else that I or anyone else could do. I didn't want her to suffer and prayed the end would come soon and without pain. Though it hurt to think I'd never hold little Emily again or walk outside in the garden with her sitting atop my shoulder I wanted her at peace. I wanted God to set her free.

In the last days I spent every spare moment I had talking to Emily. The days were now sunny and warm so we often walked around the yard and sat in the garden. All my flowers were in bloom and the weather had been so nice. Emily had always loved the warm sun on her face and even though she could no longer see she could hear the birds and other creatures all around her. She'd perk up her ears and even seemed to sense when other squirrels were nearby. Our backyard buddies came around to look at Emily curiously as she sat on my lap and I fed them their peanuts. Perhaps they sensed her failing health. I always talked to them too as if they were little people. They too were my buddies so I told them all about Emily's illness and that she would have to say goodbye to all her outdoor friends soon. Those little outdoor squirrels would be tremendous support for me when the inevitable happened and Emily was no longer with us. I had a strong feeling I would be attaching myself to all of them for comfort.

Chapter Sixteen

Sleep Sweet Emily

It hadn't been especially hot that August of 2006. The weather was sunny and dry. I was getting very weary from not sleeping and worrying about Emily. Working was difficult. My heart just wasn't in it and my thoughts were on her all the time now. I wanted to be home. I did not want her to pass away with me not there. I just wanted to be with her and prayed that's how the end would come. Even if I was asleep, at least I would be in the house and she wouldn't be alone. She would feel me there, and I'd feel better about that.

It was a Monday. I came home from work as always and the first thing I did when I came through the door was go to Emily and check on her. I took her out of her hammock and began feeding her and offering water with the eyedropper. She was very lethargic and barely responsive to me at all. Her condition had worsened and she was very weak. I knew I couldn't do enough anymore and that just made me feel angry and helpless. After all, I'd been Emily's companion and "mother" all these years. Now I felt I was letting her down. I couldn't eat or do anything that night I felt so depressed. Around dinnertime I brought Alfie out into the living room as I always did so Emily could have company during the evening hours. I watched as she seemed to sleep, but I could tell she was uncomfortable, maybe even in pain. It was very hard for me but I stroked her frail body and kept telling her how much I loved her. I told her that if she felt she couldn't hold on to just let go. Aunt Lisa, grandmom and all the family pets she shared her life with would all be waiting to greet her and that she would have no more pain and be able to run around and climb and see once again. This loss of sight had greatly troubled me. Emily had only my voice and touch to go by. I kept telling her these things over and over and somehow I think she understood what I was trying to say, in her own little squirrel way. At least my voice and touch would comfort and reassure her.

My heart was very heavy that evening. I had a strong feeling that this might be the night she would pass away and I couldn't hold back my tears, but I didn't want Emily to know how sad I felt. I've been told that pets can sense your sadness and I thought that might make it harder for her to let go. I didn't want her to try hanging on for me. I had always felt that little squirrel loved me so much.

I started to retire to my room and try and get some sleep around 11:30 that night. My trouble sleeping in the past few months had largely been due to worrying about Emily. I placed Alfie back in his room next to mine and went once more into Emily and kissed her goodnight and told her to "sleep sweet" like I always said to her every night before turning out the lights. I stood by the cage talking softly to her and I said this prayer,

"Please Lord, free Emily from her suffering. She's a small frail creature that you created...your most precious gift to me for safe keeping. I've loved her and tried my very best to take care of her all these years. I will miss her but I cannot stand to watch her suffer this way any longer. I can't bear to take her out of this house to the vet and have her put to sleep. So please, I'm asking you to take her and make her whole once more. Give her the life she was meant to live, the life she didn't get to live here on earth. I am so grateful to you Lord for letting me have Emily for so long and now I give her back to you for safe keeping until she and I can be reunited in Heaven."

Tears streamed down my face and my heart sank, but I loved her enough to let go. I went into my room and lay on the bed. Sleep would not come. I was awake the whole night but never tried to get up. I kept thinking about how horrible I would feel by morning from lack of sleep and how hard it would be to go to work. At about 6:30 a.m. I decided to get up and go into Emily. I found her at the bottom of her cage on her blankets and when I went to pick her up she was gone. My prayers had been answered and God took her that night. I never cried so hard except when I lost my parents, good friends like Lisa and previous pets. This loss would be hard to get over. I lay across my bed and held her close, crying and calling her name. I wanted her little eyes to just open for a second. I wanted her back for a brief moment just to tell her how much I loved her even though I already knew in my heart that Emily knew how much she was loved and how special she was to me. My body and mind were totally drained. I didn't know how I could muster the energy now to bury her. I had picked a special place outside my kitchen window, the same window Emily and I had stood at so many times looking out at the other animals, the snow, the rain, the sunshine and flowers. It was a sunny window and Emily's favorite place to stretch out across my arm as though it was a tree branch. I wanted to bury her in a small rock garden that I could see from that same window. There's a beautiful cherry blossom tree and come spring there would be lots of daffodils coming up. I would make sure Emily would always have flowers around her.

Chapter Seventeen

Emily's Garden and The Clock

That morning seems like a blur now but I remember
calling work and telling my boss what happened and she
was kind enough to let me have the day to mourn and do
what I needed to do. I knew I didn't have the strength to
prepare the place for Emily so I called the landscaper who
had made the flower bed for me. He was kind enough to
come out and prepare the spot for me. The small garden
outside my kitchen window would now become Emily's
final resting place. I christened the spot "Emily's Garden"
as she loved to sit there with me on the decorative
concrete bench that was held up by two concrete squirrels.
Years before I had had a talented friend fashion a small
wooden box for me for just this occasion. It was made
of sturdy mahogany hardwood and had Emily's name
and a squirrel hand painted on top. The box would last a
very long time in the soil. Now I took it out and looked
at it, tears welling up in my eyes. The time had finally
come to place her in that box and lay her down to sleep
forever in her beautiful garden for the last time. I knew
I would take all of this hard. Only those who have had
close relationships with their pets can understand what I

was going through, and I know there are many who do. Though my heart was breaking my whole experience with Emily was one I wouldn't have traded for anything in the world. I placed one of her soft fleece blankets inside the box, wrapped her in one she used to sleep in from her hammock and I laid her inside. A little heart with a rose and a picture of Emily and me that sis took when I was lying in bed with her across my chest one morning also went into the small box. I even put her favorite pecans, wrapped in a plastic bag, beside her.

Everything happened so fast that morning. I wished I hadn't buried her so soon, and that I had placed a few toys in her box. But nothing more I could've done would've lessened the pain of missing her. Keeping her an hour or so longer would've only prolonged the pain, so I closed the box and went outside to the garden and we placed Emily in the ground. I said a prayer for her and told her I would always love her and we'd be together again someday.

"I will never forget you" I said. "You will live in my heart forever. You're free now and I know you're still with me in spirit. When I sit on this bench thinking of the time we spent together you'll be right here with me on my lap with your little paws wrapped around my hands, just like before. I can almost see you running around and climbing the highest tree. No more pain! You can see again and the legs that were useless to you in life are brand new."

We covered the grave with soil and mulch and I went back inside the house. Nothing was the same. Staring at the empty cage only brought on more tears. No more would I see her little face gazing at me from over the side of her hammock. I used to call her hammock her "happy sack" and so enjoyed seeing her in it while I sat on the couch watching T.V. beside her. There was so much I was going to miss.

Not wanting to touch anything inside her cage I left things as they were for a very long time. It was a couple of months until I decided to dust everything and clean it up but I never threw away any of her toys or bedding. I put the toys in a shopping bag and kept them. The bedding was washed and put away. Maybe someday there would be another helpless little squirrel to care for. It wouldn't replace Emily but I know I'd have a hard time saying no to taking in another. To this day I sleep with one of Emily's stuffed toys and a piece of blanket she chewed holes in. I always say, "She made this for me." It was Emily's handiwork. Her own "design." In time I turned the cage into a little memorial for Emily with stuffed animals, photos, and cards that people had sent me. The cage occupies the same place in the corner of my living room next to the couch. Sometimes when I'm watching T.V. I almost think I can hear the "happy sack" move around. Maybe Emily still comes to spend time in that hammock and comfort the friend who misses her so much.

During the six months that Emily had started going downhill I found a wonderful clock in a local gift shop. The face had a French inscription, "Le Jardin D'Emilie " (The Garden of Emily). It seemed a perfect tribute to the garden she had loved, so I went back to the shop and purchased it and placed it on the wall by the back door.

The shop keeper had given me a discount on the clock as they couldn't get the pendulum to work. I, too, tried in vain to get it to work without any luck. But it kept good time and the little saying on it meant a lot to me. Then a strange thing happened. It was a couple of days after Emily had passed away. I was taking laundry down to the basement when I noticed the pendulum was swinging back and forth. Stunned, I dropped the basket of clothes and stood there watching it. I had tried for weeks to get it to move to no avail. Was this Emily's way of letting me know she's alright and happy? The thought would not escape me that maybe Emily or someone else was trying to tell me something. There was no logical reason for the pendulum to suddenly start to swing on its own. I even removed it from the wall one day to have some work done and when I put it back up it continued to work just fine. The work involved a local artist painting a beautiful mural on the wall that leads out to Emily's garden. Later I moved the clock to a place in the kitchen near the mural and to this day the pendulum continues to swing.

Chapter Eighteen

Soliloquy for Emily

Emily had been my whole world and in the days
and weeks following her death coming home to a house
without her was very difficult. Alfie missed her too I
could tell. He sensed my sadness. Sitting on the couch
and not seeing her next to me in her cage where I could
reach in and take her from the little hammock made me
feel so empty. It's been well over a year now. This will be
the second Christmas without her. I still put up a tree and
recall how Emily loved it with all the little stars decorating
it as though she was surrounded by them. I've kept her
Christmas stocking and have fond memories of how she
would pull the nuts and other goodies from inside it. I
still fill her stocking, but now I take the goodies outside
to share with all the outdoor squirrels. I think Emily
would approve. So another Christmas has come and
gone and winter is upon us once more. I look out my
kitchen window into the garden where Emily rests and
think warm thoughts of all the times we spent together
and how she made me laugh. She was definitely a stress
reliever, lightening the troubles of a work day with her cute
little antics. I still have my memories along with lots of

wonderful photos taken through the years by family and friends.

As I write this final chapter Spring is not too far away. The flowering bulbs I planted will soon be up and the gardens will come alive. I'll sit out on the concrete bench and reminisce about the times Emily sat there with me on my lap, paws neatly folded around my hands. The daffodils and lilies will look so beautiful in her garden. Emily will be part of the new life that springs forth from the soil and I'll see her image in all the squirrels running to and fro in the garden. Her spirit will always be here with me. Each year now on the anniversary of her passing I release a pink balloon into the sky to signify my on-going love and thoughts of her. One day another squirrel may enter my life, God knows there's plenty of room in my heart though Emily will always occupy a little corner of it. That is where she lives now and I think she'd be very happy knowing her cage may someday be home to another little squirrel in need. I would always welcome the opportunity to care for another one.

Till then, the outside squirrels continue to keep me company, bringing their new babies to me in spring, ever searching for a handout of nuts and other goodies. Losing Emily gave me a new family of friends, and there will always be a need in me to help the "outside buddies" who used to come up to greet her when we sat outdoors together. In a way, she is responsible for me having so many now to care for in the outside world. The need in me to care for God's lesser creatures will continue. I look at them and see my Emily, my sweet little "button nose" running happily amongst them all.   In these busy squirrels who occupy my little garden space and my world, Emily's spirit is ever present.

finis

An Acorn for Emily

An acorn fell to earth today
As if the Lord was trying to say
That I could stop my crying now
And though I can't imagine how
I know he'll help me find a way.

An acorn fell to earth today
And settled there where I had found
A sweet warm place for her to lie
So she can see the bright blue sky
And hear the rain's soft gentle sound.

In life she missed these simple things
The morning dew, the birds that sing
But she was happy just to be
A part of daily life with me
And now her soul has taken wing.

An acorn fell to earth today
And rooted there so it will stay
A mighty oak to one day be
Some shade for Emily and me.
Again we'll meet, I know she waits
With acorns there, at Heaven's gate.

Christine Rosinola Wittmann